Walt Disney's Comics and Stories
No. 660 September 2005.
Published monthly by Gemstone Publishing.
© 2005 Disney Enterprises, In., except where noted.
All rights reserved. Nothing contained herein may be reproduced
without the written permission of Disney Enterprises, Inc.,
Burbank, CA, or other copyright holders.

ISBN 0-911903-85-2

Walt Disney's DONALD DUCK

• THE IDLE GLITCH •

AH, THE BOYS ARE OFF TO GRANDMA'S FOR A **WHOLE WEEK**! A WEEK IN WHICH I'M GOING TO ELEVATE LOAFING TO A **FINE ART**!

I'M NOT GOING TO COOK OR CLEAN OR DUST, OR EXERT MYSELF IN ANY WAY IMAGINABLE!

FOR THE NEXT SEVEN DAYS MY LIFE IS GOING TO BE A MONUMENT TO THE BLISS OF **INDOLENCE**!

AND IT WILL ALL BE THANKS TO **DUCKBURG ROBOTICS, INC.**! A MERE PHONE CALL, AND A BENEDICTION OF SLOTH SHALL DESCEND UPON MY SOON TO BE SOMNOLENT BROW!

AND SO—

YOU BET, MISTER DUCK! WE CAN HAVE AN **M-16** HOUSEHOLD MODEL DELIVERED BY TWO O'CLOCK THIS AFTERNOON!

DUCKBURG ROBOTICS, INC.

SALES

TWO O'CLOCK ARRIVES PROMPTLY!

SIGN HERE, MISTER DUCK, AND **PERCY** IS YOURS FOR A WEEK!

PERCY, EH? WELL, WELL, HELLO, PERCY!

HELLO, MISTER DUCK! I AM INDEED MOST EAGER TO ASSUME MY DUTIES!

NO LESS EAGER THAN I AM, **BELIEVE** ME!

HERE'S A SPEC SHEET ON PERCY, MISTER DUCK! HE IS VOICE ACTIVATED, SELF MAINTAINING, AND PROGRAMMED TO BE A BARREL OF LAUGHS!

GOOD! HE CAN TELL ME JOKES WHILE HE PEELS ME A GRAPE!

HOUSEHOLD M-16

DUCKBURG ROBOTICS

NOW, PERCY, TO BEGIN WITH, I'D LIKE—

TUT! TUT! MERELY STAND ASIDE, MISTER DUCK! I SHALL COMMENCE FORTHWITH TO ORGANIZE YOUR DOMICILE!

ALL I HAD IN MIND IS A DISH OF **PISTACHIO!**

SIMPLICITY ITSELF!

MERCY! WHAT A **RAT'S NEST!** TIDY! TIDY! TIDY, MISTER DUCK! THAT'S OUR MOTTO!

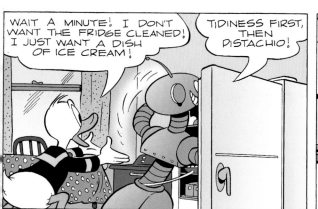

WAIT A MINUTE! I DON'T WANT THE FRIDGE CLEANED! I JUST WANT A DISH OF ICE CREAM!

TIDINESS FIRST, THEN PISTACHIO!

WELL, IT IS A MESS, I'LL ADMIT!

ONLY FOR A MOMENT MORE, YOU MAY REST ASSURED!

THERE YOU ARE, CLEAN AS A WHISTLE, AND PISTACHIO TO BOOT!

THANK YOU! I'LL JUST—

CHAIRS UP! THERE'S A FLOOR TO CLEAN! CUPBOARDS TO ORGANIZE, AND CURTAINS TO IRON!

HEY!

THUD

PLOP

OH, MESSY MESSY, MISTER DUCK! YOU REALLY SHOULD TRY **EATING** YOUR PISTACHIO! IT'S SO MUCH MORE **TIDY** THAT WAY!

HEY! **OW!** QUIT ALREADY! I CAN CLEAN OFF MY **OWN** HEAD!

MAYBE I'M BETTER OFF OUT OF THE KITCHEN! LEAVE IT TO PERCY! THAT **IS** THE WHOLE IDEA, AFTER ALL!

THIS IS NUTS! IF I CAN'T USE THE PHONE, I GUESS I'LL HAVE TO GO DOWN TO DUCKBURG ROBOTICS **IN PERSON!**

BACK OFF! I'VE JUST **POLISHED THE KNOBS!**

ZIP

WAIT A MINUTE! WHAT GOOD ARE DOORS IF I CAN'T **OPEN** THEM?

BESIDES—THEY'RE **MY** DOORS!

BUT THEIR MAINTENANCE IS **MY** RESPONSIBILITY! NOW MOVE ALONG! I HAVE FLOORS TO VACUUM!

YOICKS! I'M A PRISONER IN MY OWN HOME! I WONDER IF THERE'S SOME WAY TO **SHORT CIRCUIT** THIS METAL MONSTER?

MEANWHILE, THERE IS GREAT DISMAY AT DUCKBURG ROBOTICS, INC.!

COME AGAIN?

THE M-16**X** IS **MISSING**, SIR! IT MUST HAVE BEEN SENT OUT ON A JOB BY **MISTAKE!**

YOU MEAN TO TELL ME THAT AN **EXPERIMENTAL** ROBOT PROGRAMMED TO TAKE CARE OF **200 UNIT HOTELS** HAS BEEN SENT OUT ON A ROUTINE **SINGLE UNIT** ASSIGNMENT?

APPARENTLY SO, SIR!

WELL **FIND** IT! THE M-16X WILL RUN AMOK TRYING TO FULFILL ITS ACCELERATED PROGRAM!

IF IT WRECKS SOMEONE'S HOME, WE'LL BE SUED FOR OUR **BACK TEETH!**

YES, SIR! VERY GOOD, SIR!

AND SO, AS THE EVENING SHADOWS FALL—

HOME AT LAST!

AND A DAY EARLY!

UNCA DONALD WON'T MIND! AFTER ALL, HE'S HAD SIX DAYS OF CREATIVE LOAFING!

HEY! WHO'S THIS GUY?

LOOKS LIKE A DOCTOR OF SOME KIND!

NOW WHAT?

THE DOCTOR EXPLAINS!

YEAH, BUT WHAT ACTUALLY HAPPENED TO UNCA DONALD?

I HAVE NO IDEA! HE WAS DISCOVERED EARLIER TODAY RUNNING IN CIRCLES IN THE FRONT YARD BABBLING ABOUT BEING FREE!

AND YOU SAY HE HAS TO BE ON BED REST FOR A WHOLE MONTH?

THAT'S RIGHT, BOYS! YOUR UNCLE IS SUFFERING FROM TOTAL EXHAUSTION! HE IS TO DO NOTHING MORE THAN ACT LIKE A POLYP!

A MONTH? CRIMINEY! THAT MEANS WE'LL HAVE TO DO EVERYTHING AROUND HERE!

GROAN!

MAYBE NOT, GUYS! LOOK AT THIS!

"DUCKBURG ROBOTICS, INC., HOUSEKEEPING ROBOTS"!

SO WHAT?

SO MAYBE WE COULD RENT ONE!

AND SO, AS THE EVENING SHADOWS FALL—

HOME AT LAST!

AND A **DAY** EARLY!

UNCA DONALD WON'T MIND! AFTER ALL, HE'S HAD **SIX DAYS** OF CREATIVE LOAFING!

HEY! WHO'S THIS GUY?

LOOKS LIKE A **DOCTOR** OF SOME KIND!

NOW WHAT?

THE DOCTOR EXPLAINS!

YEAH, BUT WHAT ACTUALLY **HAPPENED** TO UNCA DONALD?

I HAVE NO IDEA! HE WAS DISCOVERED EARLIER TODAY RUNNING IN CIRCLES IN THE FRONT YARD BABBLING ABOUT BEING **FREE**!

AND YOU SAY HE HAS TO BE ON BED REST FOR A **WHOLE MONTH**?

THAT'S RIGHT, BOYS! YOUR UNCLE IS SUFFERING FROM TOTAL EXHAUSTION! HE IS TO DO NOTHING MORE THAN ACT LIKE A **POLYP**!

A MONTH? CRIMINEY! THAT MEANS WE'LL HAVE TO DO **EVERYTHING** AROUND HERE!

GROAN!

MAYBE NOT, GUYS! LOOK AT THIS!

"DUCKBURG ROBOTICS, INC., HOUSEKEEPING ROBOTS"!

SO WHAT?

SO MAYBE WE COULD **RENT** ONE!

STOP, THIEF...OR PLUTO WILL SEE THAT YOU **DO**!

PLUTO!

HEADING FOR THE UNDERWORLD WON'T DO THE LITTLE ROBBER ANY GOOD!

NOT WHEN PEERLESS PLUTO'S ON HIS TAIL... ER...TRAIL!

?

QUIT DIGGING UP MY SHRUBS, YOU MUTT!

THIS **WAS** A PRIZE ORNAMENTAL! NOW IT'S RUINED! RUINED!

I'M SORRY, MR. MUGGINS! PLUTO DIDN'T MEAN TO DIG IT UP!

I'LL PAY FOR IT! JUST SEND ME THE BILL!

HUMPH!

PLUTO, I WISH YOU'D PLEASE TRY TO BE A GOOD DOG!

I CAN'T KEEP TRACK OF YOU AND MY COLLECTIONS, TOO!

LET'S SEE NOW... I LEFT THE BUCKET RIGHT HERE...

PEERLESS PLUTO TAKES THE CASE!

THE YARDS! WHAT A PLACE! LIKE TRYING TO FIND A NOODLE IN A HEMSTITCH!

NO! THERE HE IS! ON THAT BRIDGE, CROSSING THE TRACKS!

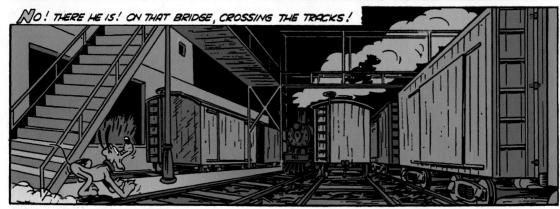

OH, NO, YOU DON'T, MR. BUCKET-BURGLAR...

THIS IS ONE BUCKET YOU'RE NOT GETTING AWAY WITH!

And for once, Pluto's RIGHT!

BONK!

OOF!

Who cares if the crook's getting away with the money? Pluto's got stars in his eyes!

He's walking on air!

TWEET! TWEET!

Oops! For a while he was, anyway!

PLOK!

Down he goes ...right into a refrigerator car!

THAT'S IT, JOE! LOCK 'EM UP!

RIGHT!

TWEET! TWEET!

Whoa! Looks like Pluto's on ice for this trip!

O-O-OH! EVERYTHING GONE! BOO HOO HOO! ...AND NO SIGN OF PLUTO!

Next morning! Three hundred miles later...

HEY! LOOK WHAT I FOUND!

MIGOSH! IT'S SHAPED SOMETHING LIKE A DOG! MAYBE IT IS ONE!

C'MON! LET'S THAW IT OUT OVER AT THE CAFÉ ...AND FIND OUT FOR SURE!

TRACK CAFÉ

CAFÉ

CAFÉ

WELL, AT LEAST HE DIDN'T HAVE TO TRAVEL IN THE ICEBOX...AND THAT MEANS A LOT!

ARF!

PLUTO! WELCOME HOME, FELLA!

WE HEARD WHAT YOU DID, PLUTO!

PAPERS AND MAGAZINES

HERE YOU ARE, MISS MINNIE! YOUR CHARITY COLLECTIONS! KEH ...OF COURSE, THE BOYS IN THE POLICE DEPARTMENT ADDED A BIT!

OH, THANK YOU! THANK YOU! AND TO THINK, IF IT HADN'T BEEN FOR PLUTO...

YOU DON'T KNOW THE HALF OF IT! HE EVEN MANAGED TO GET BACK A FEW OTHER THINGS AND EARN HIMSELF THIS REWARD!

GOSH! IMAGINE THAT!

WELL, OL' BOY...WHAT WOULD YOU DO WITH ALL THIS MONEY IF WE GAVE IT RIGHT TO YOU? HERE! WANT TO HOLD IT FOR A WHILE!

!

WHY... WHAT DO Y' KNOW! HE MUST WANT TO GIVE IT TO YOUR CHARITY DRIVE, MINNIE!

SPLUT! SPLUT!

MY GOODNESS! DO YOU THINK HE REALLY UNDERSTANDS ABOUT SUCH THINGS?

SNORT!

PERSONALLY, HE THINKS IT TASTES AWFUL!

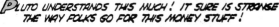

PLUTO UNDERSTANDS THIS MUCH! IT SURE IS STRANGE THE WAY FOLKS GO FOR THIS MONEY STUFF!

GEMSTONE PUBLISHING
presents
YOUR FAVORITE DISNEY COMICS

© 2005 Disney
Enterprises Inc.

Delivered right to your door!

We know how much you enjoy visiting your local comic shop, but wouldn't it be nice to have your favorite Disney comics delivered to you? Subscribe today and we'll send the latest issues of your favorite comics directly to your doorstep. And if you would still prefer to browse through the latest in comic art but aren't sure where to go, check out the Comic Shop Locator Service at www.diamondcomics.com/csls or call 1-888-COMIC-BOOK.

Walt Disney's MICKEY MOUSE and DONALD DUCK in

MYTHOS ISLAND: CHAPTER 7
SEARCHING FOR THE GIRLS

OUR POOR SHIPWRECKED PALS HAVE MANAGED TO MANGLE A PLANE, A BOAT AND A HYDROFOIL TO BECOME MAROONED ON THIS MYSTERIOUS ISLE! HOW THEY FOUND MYTHOS ISLAND IS ONE STORY AND HOW THEY'RE GOING TO GET BACK HOME IS QUITE ANOTHER...

DONALD, YOU INSUFFERABLE IDLER! GET UP! OUR ESCAPE CRAFT WON'T BUILD ITSELF!

UUNGH...!!

‡YAWN!‡ TH' BREAKFAST FISHIES WON'T BE CATCHIN' THEIRSELVES, NEITHER!

D 2002-231

‡GRUMBLE!‡ WHAT A MISERABLE FIX, UNCLE SCROOGE! IF YOU'RE NOT ORDERING ME AROUND, THEN MICKEY IS!

QUIT GRIPING! YOU WANT TO GET BACK TO YOUR SWEETIE, DON'T YOU?

OH, YEAH... DAISY! I HAD THE MOST LIFE-LIKE DREAM ABOUT HER LAST NIGHT!

THAT'S FUNNY! I DREAMT ABOUT MINNIE, TOO!

SHE SEEMED SO CLOSE! BUT THAT'S SILLY! OUR DOLLS ARE THOUSANDS OF MILES AWAY...

...PROBABLY GOING NUTS WITH WORRY ABOUT US!

BANG!

MICKEY AND DONALD DON'T KNOW HOW WRONG THEY ARE! THE GIRLS ARE JUST A FEW HUNDRED FEET AWAY...

WAKE UP, MINNIE! WE FELL ASLEEP!

NO WONDER, DAISY! THIS JOURNEY HAS BEEN SIMPLY EXHAUSTING!

BUT IT'S BEEN WORTH IT! ALL WE HAVE TO DO IS GET DOWN THAT SLOPE AND JOIN THE BOYS!

HOPEFULLY, THEY'VE FIGURED OUT A WAY TO GET OFF THIS ISLAN—HEY! WHAT'S HAPPENING?

RRUMBLE...

ANOTHER AVALANCHE! STICK TO THE CLIFF SO THE ROCKS WON'T HIT US!

YIKES! THE WHOLE MOUNTAIN'S SHAKING!

RRUMBLE!

GOODNESS GRACIOUS! LET'S NOT PANIC, DAISY!

WHY NOT?! THERE'S NOTHING ELSE WE CAN DO!

KLAK! AK!

CRACK!

I KNOW THE BOYS ARE TOO FAR AWAY... BUT I FEEL LIKE SCREAMING!

LET'S TRY IT! MAYBE PLUTO WILL HEAR US!

O MY STARS AND GARTERS! ANOTHER ROCKSLIDE! NEXT TO THAT WATERFALL!

THEY'RE GETTING TOO CLOSE FOR COMFORT!

RRUMBLE!

WHINE...

WE CAN'T LEAVE THE SHORE! WE'VE GOTTA FINISH BUILDING AN ESCAPE CRAFT OUT OF SALVAGED PARTS!

WHAT'S THE POINT?! YOUR DESIGN WILL SINK LIKE A STONE, MOUSE!

OH YEAH?! IF I LEFT IT TO YOU, WE'D END UP PUTTING OUT TO SEA IN A COFFEE GRINDER!

GAWRSH! LOOKIT WHUT I CAUGHT, FELLAHS!

THANKS FER TH' COMPLIMENT, SIR! NOW LET'S GO FIND THEM GALS!

OF COURSE! BUT ALONG THE WAY...

...BE SURE TO KEEP YOUR EYES OPEN FOR ANY VALUABLE NATURAL RESOURCES WE MIGHT STUMBLE ACROSS!

YIKES! WHUT'S HAP- PENIN'?

RRUMBLE!

CRACK!

CRIMINY! WE BETTER GIT MOVIN'!

SPLASH!

RRUMBLE!

WAK! GOOFY! YOU SAVED MY TAIL- FEATHERS!

UHF!

BUMP!

GOOFY! ARE YOU ALL RIGHT?!

YUP! AN' LOOK WHUT I FOUND DOWN HERE!

A GIGANTIC DIAMOND?! I TAKE BACK WHAT I SAID! YOU'RE THE BEST PARTNER A MAN COULD HAVE!

MEAN-WHILE...

DAISY! TH- THE BOYS' CAMP HAS VANISHED!

BUT THEY ALL MANAGED TO GET AWAY...DIDN'T THEY?!

OH MY! LOOK WHO'S HERE!!

THE LITTLE MECHANICAL FAIRY!

SWISH!

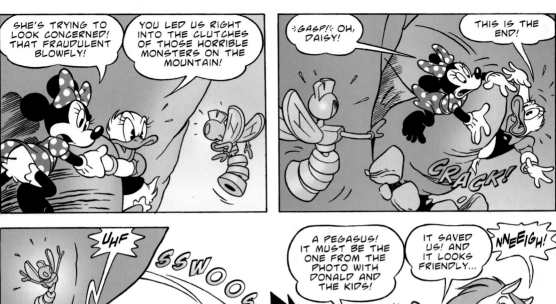

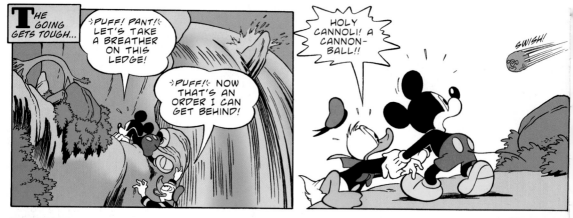

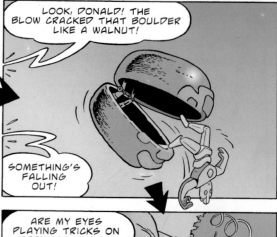

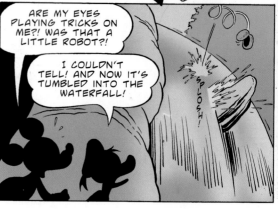

BUT *RIDDLES* ARE WHAT YOU DO BEST!

AND I'VE GOT *SUCH* A GOOD ONE TOO! OH, ALL RIGHT! ⇥*GIGGLE!*⇤ NOW LISTEN UP...

WHAT CREATURE GOES ON FOUR FEET IN THE MORNING, ON TWO FEET AT NOON, AND ON THREE FEET IN THE EVENING?

GEE, IS THAT THE *BEST* YOU CAN DO?!

THE ANSWER IS... *MAN!* AS A CHILD, HE CREEPS ON HIS HANDS AND KNEES...

...AS AN ADULT, HE WALKS ERECT...

...AND IN OLD AGE, HE HOBBLES ALONG USING A CANE!

AND IN TWO SHAKES OF A DUCK'S TAIL...

OH, THESE GOSH-DARNED EDUCATED KIDS TODAY!

WH!NE!

MEAN-WHILE...

⇥*WHEEZE!*⇤ ⇥*HUFF!*⇤ I'M OUTTA THET CREVASSE AT LAST! AN' SO'S TH' DIAMOND!

THE STONE IS *FANTASTIC!* I *KNEW* I'D FIND A FORTUNE ON THIS ISLAND!

NOW HOLD ON A GOLDURNED MINUTE! WASN'T IT *ME* THET FOUND IT?!

WE'LL HAGGLE OVER PARTICULARS LATER! LET'S PUSH ON! THE SHORE-LINE'S CRUMBLING UNDER OUR FEET!

CUSHLAMACREE!!

MR. McDUCK!

SWOOSH!

TOM? NO? DICK? NO? HARRY?

OH, FORGET IT! WE MIGHT JUST AS WELL GIVE UP!

BAH! IT'S JUST LIKE MY FRIEND MIGHTOS SAID! YOU DON'T KNOW MY NAME!

THEREFORE, YOU SHALL TASTE MY CLUB!

WAIT! YOUR NAME IS ON THE TIP OF MY TONGUE! GIVE ME A HINT!

HMMPH! SNATCHED BY A ROC! *NOTHING* ON THIS ISLAND SURPRISES ME ANYMORE!

HEY! I GRABBED YOU OFF THAT BEACH RIGHT BEFORE IT WAS SWALLOWED BY THE SEA! YOU'RE LUCKY I CAME ALONG!

FLAP FLAP

HOLY HANNAH! IN- CREASE THE ALTITUDE, YOU FEATHER-BRAINED BEHEMOTH! WE ALMOST BUMPED INTO *FACHAN*!

SWOOSH!

YOU KNOW ME?! YOU'RE A SCOTSMAN TOO?

WHAT ARE SCROOGE AND GOOFY DOING UP THERE?! THINGS ARE GOING FROM WEIRD TO WEIRDER!

WHAT DID YOUR UNCLE CALL THIS LUG?! "FACHAN"?!

BEATS ME! NEVER HEARD OF... MMRFF!

OF COURSE! FACHAN! GOOD OL' FACHAN! *EVERYBODY* KNOWS FACHAN!

I KNEW IT! I'M JUST AS WELL KNOWN AS THAT STUPID ROC! OR ANY OF THE OTHER JOKERS ON THIS ISLAND!

FACHAN! YOU DA MAN!

HEY! IT'S THE MECHANICAL FAIRY! SHE'S TALKING TO OUR NEWEST BEST FRIEND!

BEEP! BEEP BOOP! BEEEP!

OKEE-DOKE! LEMME GET RID OF THIS FIRST!

HOLD THE PHONE! WHY ARE YOU PICKING US UP, FACHAN?!

JUST FOLLOWING ORDERS!

KA-LONK!

LISTEN, PAL! WE'RE ⇒UHF!⇐ SEARCHING FOR OUR ⇒UHF!⇐ GIRLFRIENDS! WHY ARE YOU ⇒UHF!⇐ HOPPING AWAY WITH US?!

YOU'LL SEE!

HOP!

HOP!

MEANWHILE...

THERE GO THE TROLLS! THEY'RE HEADING FOR THAT STRANGE TEMPLE NEAR THE MOUNTAIN TOP!

TSK! SILLY TROLLS! YOU'VE GOTTEN INTO OUR MAKEUP! AND MY SPARE DRESS IS RUINED!

YOU WERE SUPPOSED TO FETCH OUR LUGGAGE, NOT PLAY WITH IT!

WE SHOULD HAVE GUESSED! IF WE EVER NEED TROLL TAMERS, YOU'RE HIRED!

HUEY! DEWEY! LOUIE! AND PLUTO!

UNCLE SCROOGE, DONALD, MICKEY AND GOOFY?! WHERE ARE THEY?

LOOK!

WHAT TOOK YOU SO LONG, ROCCY-BOY?!

PHEW! I'M NO SPRING CHICKEN! I HAD TO TAKE A COUPLE OF BREAKS ON THE WAY UP!

HOP!

HOP!

BUMP!

I'VE GOT YOU ALL TOGETHER AT LAST! GREETINGS, STRANGERS! AS YOU MAY HAVE GUESSED, THIS ISLAND IS THE HOME OF ALL THE **WORLD'S MYTHOLOGICAL CREATURES!**

YOU'VE MET AIRY, MY ASSISTANT! SHE'S DONE HER BEST TO MAKE YOU FEEL WELCOME HERE!

I'M MASTER MYTHOS AND I RUN THIS LITTLE ENTERPRISE!

SADLY, I'VE HAD SOME TROUBLE WITH MIGHTOS—FORMERLY MY LITTLE HELPER—WHO CONVINCED A FEW OF MY SUBJECTS THAT YOU WERE HOSTILE INTRUDERS!

HE'S STILL OUT THERE... BUT A FAR GRAVER PROBLEM IS AT HAND! ONE THAT CONCERNS THE FATE OF THE ENTIRE ISLAND! IN THE MEANTIME...

"...WELCOME! YOU'RE AMONG FRIENDS!"

I LOST YOUR BEAT UP SHOE, MINNIE, BUT HERE'S ANOTHER ONE FROM YOUR SUITCASE!

PEGGY!

I'M SURE GLAD I PACKED A SPARE BOW!

WITH OR WITHOUT IT, DOLL, YOU'RE A SIGHT FOR SORE EYES!

Continued in this issue..

DULL KINDA DANGER

ANOTHER POST CARD FROM YOUR GRAN'DADDY, CHIP 'N' DALE, AND, AS USUAL, HE WRITES THE USUAL-TYPE MESSAGE!

UH-HUH! WE KNOW...USUAL DULL STUFF LIKE "THINGS ARE GOING ON AS ALWAYS... NORMAL WEATHER, ETC!"

CHIP 'N' DALE

MAIL

POOR OL' GRAN'DADDY SURE LEADS AN UNEXCITING KINDA LIFE!

SAY, YOU KNOW, WE NEVER *HAVE* VISITED GRAN'DADDY'S HOUSE! HE ALWAYS WRITES AND SAYS "DON'T BOTHER... I'LL COME TO *YOUR* PLACE!"

MAYBE HE'S AFRAID WE'D FIND THINGS TOO DULL AT HIS PLACE!

WELL, I THINK IT'S TIME WE PAY HIM A SURPRISE VISIT!

OKAY! WE GOT HIS *ADDRESS!* SHOULDN'T BE HARD TO FIND!

So...

HI-HO... IT'S OFF TO PEP-UP GRAN'PAPPY'S LIFE WE GO... ♫♪♪ ♫♪

AHA! HERE'S GRAN'DADDY'S STREET! WE TURN HERE!

LONE TREE ROAD

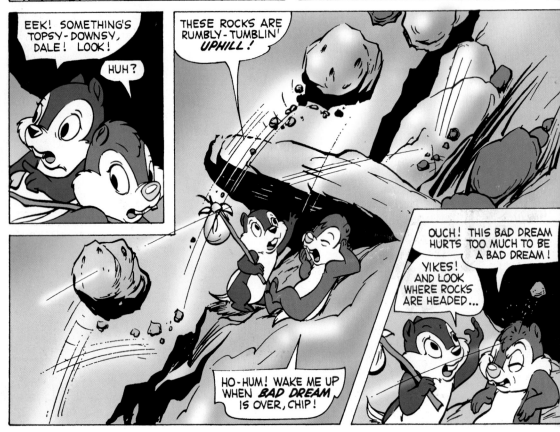

THEY'RE ALL BULL'S-EYE-LIKE BASHIN' INTO GRAN'DADDY'S LONE HOME TREE!

GRANDADDY

BLAM!

BASH!

OH, HOW AWFUL!

C'MON! ROCKS STOPPED! LET'S SEE IF GRAN'DADDY'S *OKAY* OR...OR *KAYOED!*

SAY, THAT'S A QUEERLY KINDA CLOUD CLUSTERING UP ABOVE!

THERE WAS NOTHING THERE A SECOND AGO!

KA-BOOM! SPLASH! CRASH!

EEK! NEVER SAW SUCHA STORM!

GRANDADDY

IT'S PART *LIGHTNING*, PART *FIRE*, AND PART *HOT RAIN!*

IT...IT'S ALL OVER ALL OF A SUDDEN!

QUICK...GOTTA RESCUE GRAN'PAPPY BEFORE THERE'S ANOTHER CHANGE INNA WEATHER!

EEK! HE'S OUT COLD!

(GRUMBLE!) WEEPIN' WILLOWS! WHO'S YELPIN' AND RUININ' MY NAP?

Y-YOU WERE NAPPING THROUGH ALL *THAT*?!

CHIP 'N' DALE...YOU SHOULDN'T HAVE COME HERE!

WELL, IT'S LUCKY THING WE DID! YOUR DULL DAYS ARE OVER!

WAIT... NO-NO... STOP...

WE'RE TAKING YOU HOME WITH US WHERE THE EXCITEMENT ISN'T SO GIANT-SIZED!

YOU FOOLS! I WAS SAFE IN THERE! LOOK AT MY TREE ...IT'S WICKED-WITCH-PROOF! NOTHING SHE DOES HURTS IT!

HUH? OH, GOSH... AND HERE SHE COMES!

:CHUCKLE!: AT LAST, I'VE DRIVEN YOU OUT, YOU PEST!

YOU'VE MADE A FOOL OF ME LONG ENOUGH IN YOUR LUCKY, MAGIC TREE! NOW I'LL BRING DOWN THE MOST AWFUL OF AWFULS ON YOU!

LET'S SEE NOW... EXACTLY WHAT WOULD THAT BE?

ER...IT'D BE PRETTY AWFUL IF YOU MADE IT RAIN *WALNUTS* THE SIZE OF *WATERMELONS*!

WHY, SO IT WOULD!

HO, HO! I'M SAFE AND SOUND IN MY MAGIC WITCH-PROOF TREE AGAIN!

GRRR! I'LL NEVER GIVE UP... NEVER!

GRAN'DADDY

SHE'S GOING UP TO UNLEASH MORE WITCHCRAFT! BUT IT'S NO USE... THIS TREE'S FOOLPROOF... A GIFT FROM THE GOOD FAIRY!

SEE? IT'S RAININ' ROUGH STUFF AGAIN! THIS KEEPS THE WITCH SO BUSY SHE DOESN'T HAVE TIME FOR OTHER WICKED DOINGS!

A GOOD CAUSE! BUT ...ER, HOW DO WE GET SAFELY HOME?

EASY! UNDERGROUND GOPHER TRAILS TO THE LOWLANDS! IT'S THE WAY I ALWAYS LEAVE TO VISIT YOU!

WELL, 'BYE, GRAN'DADDY!

AND WRITE OFTEN!

DOWN 'N' OUT

AND LATER, BACK HOME...

ANOTHER POST CARD FROM YOUR GRAN'DADDY, CHIP 'N' DALE!

LIKE USUAL, IT SAYS... "THINGS ARE GOIN' ON AS ALWAYS! SAME OL' TYPICAL WEATHER, DAY AND NIGHT! JUST ROUTINE-TYPE STUFF!"

¦SHUDDER!¦ ISN'T THAT JUST AWFUL-AWFUL!?!

BRRR! GIVES ME THE WILLIES AND KNEE-KNOCKS WITH TOOTH-CHATTERS!

?

CHIPMUNKS ARE HARD NUTS TO UNDERSTAND!

WALT DISNEY'S
DONALD DUCK in BETWEEN TWO WORLDS

HAVE YOU EVER WONDERED IF SOMEWHERE OUT THERE, SOMEONE JUST LIKE YOU IS LIVING IN A WORLD JUST LIKE YOURS? DO YOU BELIEVE IN ALTERNATE REALITIES—PARALLEL UNIVERSES IDENTICAL TO OUR OWN, YET EVER-SO-SLIGHTLY...DIFFERENT? AND WHAT DO YOU THINK WOULD HAPPEN IF THESE TWO WORLDS CROSSED PATHS? WELL, SOMETIMES THE STRANGEST ADVENTURES BEGIN IN THE MOST ORDINARY WAYS! ONE SUNDAY AT DUCKBURG HARBOR...

WOW! YOU'RE RIGHT, UNCA DONALD! TOURING THAT *OLD AIRCRAFT CARRIER* IS GONNA BE *WAY COOLER* THAN RIDING THE ROLLERCOASTER AT THE THRILLS 'N' SPILLS AMUSEMENT PARK!

LOOK AT THE *SIZE* OF THAT THING! LIKE A *FLOATING AIRPORT!*

AND LOOK AT THE CROWD OF LOCAL YOKELS WAITING FOR THE TOUR!

D 2003-042

HURRY UP OR WE'LL BE LATE!

I TOLD YOU, ROLLERCOASTERS ARE FOR *SISSIES!* MILITARY HISTORY IS FOR HE-DUCKS!

I'VE WATCHED SO MANY *HISTORY DOCUMENTARIES,* I BET I COULD LAND A PLANE ON HER DECK IN *ONE TRY!* URK!

STOP PUSHING! YOU'RE ABOUT 60 YEARS TOO LATE TO ENLIST ON THIS TUB!

YOU'RE WORSE THAN MY NEPHEWS! COOL YOUR JETS!

LADIES AND GENTLEMEN, PLEASE BE PATIENT!

YEAH— WHAT THE MAN SAID!

EXCUSE MY FELLOW DUCKBURGIANS, ADMIRAL! THEY'RE ALL WANNA-BE SAILORS AND PILOTS! HA, HA!

I'M NOT AN *ADMIRAL!* AND PLEASE GET BACK IN LINE WITH THE OTHERS, SIR!

NOW FOLLOW YOUR GUIDES CLOSELY AND STAY WITH YOUR GROUP...

AND ABOVE ALL, *DON'T TOUCH ANYTHING!*

YOU HEARD WHAT THE ADMIRAL SAID, KIDS! DON'T TOUCH *ANYTHING!*

I JUST *TOLD* YOU, I'M *NOT* AN *ADMIRAL!*

DON'T WORRY, I'M SURE YOU'LL GET A PROMOTION *SOONER OR LATER!*

HMPH! MOVE IT, DUCK! YOU'RE HOLDING UP THE LINE!

COME ON, BOYS! STOP BOTHERING THE CREW!

LATER...

CAREFUL, KIDS! YOU BREAK IT YOU PAY FOR IT! AND YOU KNOW WHAT EVEN A *TOILET SEAT* COSTS ON A MILITARY BUDGET!

EH? WHAT'S THIS?

KREEK!

KREEK!

AND THIS...?

KLACK!

KLACK!

ISN'T THAT SOMETHING! THEY PRESERVED IT LIKE A *MUSEUM PIECE!*

IF I WAS BORN A FEW DECADES EARLIER, I WOULD HAVE PILOTED ONE OF THESE!

VROOM! VROOM! I'LL GET YOU, CRIMSON BARON!

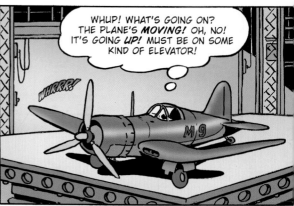

WHUP! WHAT'S GOING ON? THE PLANE'S *MOVING!* OH, NO! IT'S GOING *UP!* MUST BE ON SOME KIND OF ELEVATOR!

WHRRR!

AND NOW, CITIZENS OF DUCKBURG, FOR THE HIGHLIGHT OF OUR PROGRAM! ON THE FLIGHT DECK BEFORE YOU IS A *VINTAGE WARBIRD*—NOW CONTROLLED *ENTIRELY* BY RADIO!

IF SHE HAD SOME JUICE IN HER, I'D IMPRESS THOSE LANDLUBBERS WITH SOME LOOP-DE-LOOPS!

I COULDN'T UNDERSTAND A WORD OF WHAT THAT LOUDSPEAKER SAID, BUT I BETTER STAY HIDDEN! THEY WOULDN'T UNDERSTAND THAT I'M THE DUCK WHO CAN BEST APPRECIATE A CLOSE-UP OF THIS COCKPIT!

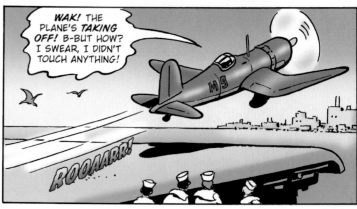

WAK! THE PLANE'S *TAKING OFF!* B-BUT HOW? I SWEAR, I DIDN'T TOUCH ANYTHING!

ROOAARR!

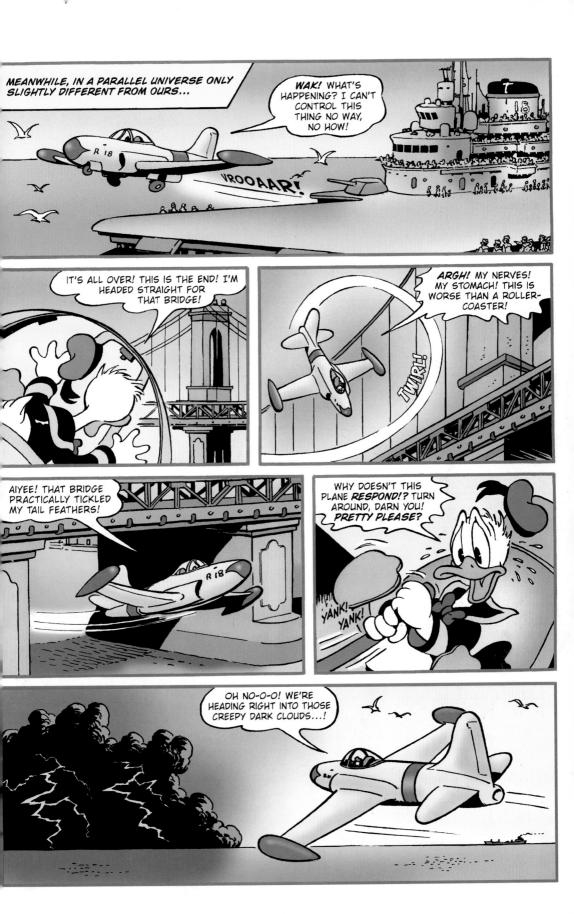

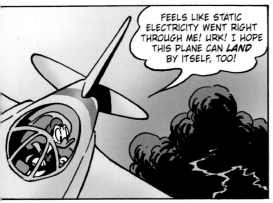

AAAGH! AND I HATE RERUNS!

LET ME OUTTA HERE!

I'M TOO OLD FOR THRILL RIDES! STOP, I WANNA GET OFF!

I PROMISE I'LL NEVER STOW AWAY IN ANOTHER AIRPLANE AGAIN! I WON'T EVEN TOUCH MY NEPHEWS' MODEL PLANES!

OKAY, OKAY! I'LL NEVER WATCH AN OLD NEWSREEL AGAIN! JUST MAKE IT STOP!

THROW ME IN THE BRIG AND FEED ME BREAD AND SEAWEED! JUST BRING ME DOWN TO SWEET MOTHER EARTH!

SPEAKING OF RERUNS... THERE'S THAT FUNNY STORM CLOUD AGAIN!

LOOKS LIKE THOSE OMINOUS CLOUDS HAVEN'T MOVED AN INCH!

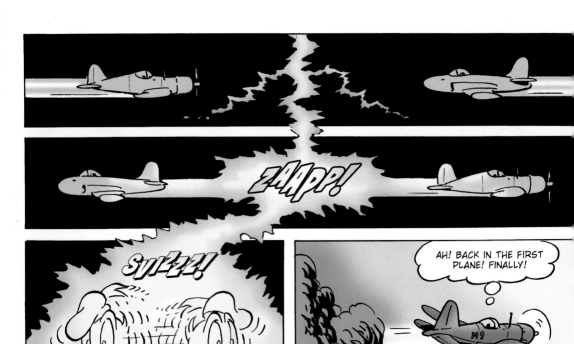

ZAAPP!

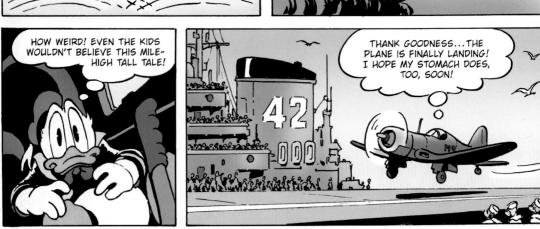

SYIZZZ!

AH! BACK IN THE FIRST PLANE! FINALLY!

HOW WEIRD! EVEN THE KIDS WOULDN'T BELIEVE THIS MILE-HIGH TALL TALE!

THANK GOODNESS...THE PLANE IS FINALLY LANDING! I HOPE MY STOMACH DOES, TOO, SOON!

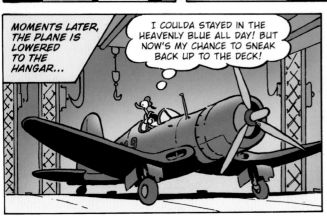

MOMENTS LATER, THE PLANE IS LOWERED TO THE HANGAR...

I COULDA STAYED IN THE HEAVENLY BLUE ALL DAY! BUT NOW'S MY CHANCE TO SNEAK BACK UP TO THE DECK!

I'VE GOT TO FIND THE BOYS FAST! THEY'LL BE WORRIED SICK!

THERE HE IS! WE FINALLY FOUND HIM!

UNCA DONALD! UNCA DONALD!

WE SEARCHED *EVERYWHERE* FOR YOU! WHERE'VE YOU BEEN?

OH, JUST TAKING A WARBIRD FOR A SPIN...

OH, SURE... LISTEN, UNCA DONALD, WE HAVE TO GET OFF THE SHIP NOW! THE OPEN HOUSE IS OVER!

SO *REALLY*, UNCA DONALD... WHAT DID YOU SEE?

MORE ACTION THAN YOU YOUNGSTERS CAN IMAGINE...

I BET YOU DIDN'T SEE ANYTHING AS COOL AS *WE* DID!

YOU DON'T KNOW WHAT YOU *MISSED!*

WE SAW A *REAL VINTAGE PLANE* FLYING *ENTIRELY* BY *RADIO CONTROL!* IT WAS REALLY SOMETHING!

ARE YOU OKAY, UNCA DONALD? WHAT'S THE MATTER?

N-NOTHING... IT'S JUST THAT... ALL OF A SUDDEN MY *SHIRT* IS TOO *TIGHT!* AND MY *HAT'S* TOO *SMALL*, TOO! I DON'T GET IT...

MEANWHILE, IN A PARALLEL DIMENSION...

I CAN'T FIGURE IT OUT, BOYS! SUDDENLY MY *SHIRT'S* TOO BIG! AND MY *HAT*, TOO!

GYRO GEARLOOSE and DOC STATIC in THE INVENTORS' TASK

GYRO GEARLOOSE AND DOC STATIC ATTEND THE ANNUAL SCIENCE EXPO AS USUAL...BUT NEITHER ONE HAS A NEW INVENTION TO SHOW!

I PLANNED AN EXHIBIT TO KNOCK FOLKS' SOCKS OFF, BUT JUST DIDN'T HAVE TIME TO GET THAT DARN MATTER TRANSPORTER WORKING RIGHT!

REASSEMBLING MATTER IS TRICKY! I WAS *THIS* CLOSE TO PERFECTING THE TECHNOLOGY MYSELF!

D 2002-249

SIGH! I GUESS THE EXPO'LL HAVE TO GO ON WITHOUT US FOR ONCE!

IT'S TOO DEPRESSING! LET'S GET OUT OF HERE! COME OVER TO...

...MY LAB AND I'LL SHOW YOU THE *NEW* INVENTION I'M WORKING ON! MAYBE THAT'LL CHEER US UP!

A PASSENGER ROCKET?! *VERY* INTERESTING! HAS IT BEEN TESTED YET?!

ALAS, NO! MICKEY MOUSE IS THE ONLY TEST PILOT I TRUST...

...BUT HE SEEMS TO HAVE *DISAPPEARED* FROM THE FACE OF THE EARTH!

THAT'S ODD! THE SAME GOES FOR DONALD AND THE BOYS!

WE COULD USE MY NEW ROCKET, GYRO! IT HASN'T BEEN TESTED, BUT...

I TRUST YOU, DOC!

I'M AFRAID THERE ISN'T MUCH ROOM! IT'S ONLY MEANT TO HOLD A SMALL PILOT AND SOME SUPPLIES!

DON'T WORRY! WE'LL SQUEEZE IN!

ZOUNDS! WHAT ACCELERATION!

NOW LET'S FIND THAT FLYING ROCK!

SWOOSH!

WHAT IF IT'S FROM ANOTHER PLANET... AND IS ON ITS WAY HOME?!

I'VE LOCATED IT ON RADAR! GOOD NEWS! IT'S STAYING WITHIN THE ATMOSPHERE!

I'LL LOCK OUR NAVIGATION SYSTEM ON TO THE FLYING BOULDER! THAT WAY WE'LL FOLLOW IT AUTOMATICALLY!

CLICK!

I HOPE MY LITTLE HELPER IS STILL HANGING ON TO THAT THING... WHATEVER IT IS!

WHOEVER INVENTED THAT OVERSIZED AIRBORNE MARBLE MUST BE A TECHNOLOGICAL WHIZ... JUST LIKE US!

AFTER HOURS OF RAPID FLIGHT OVER THE OCEAN, DOC'S ROCKET HAS PENETRATED A THICK FOG BANK...

GREAT TESLA'S COILS! WHAT KIND OF PLACE IS THIS?!

AN ISLAND! AND IT'S RAPIDLY COMING APART AT THE SEAMS!

THOSE CREATURES BELOW! THEY'RE NOT HUMAN! BUT THEY DON'T LOOK LIKE ORDINARY ANIMALS EITHER!

ULP! GYRO! WE'RE LOSING ALTITUDE FAST!

I'M AFRAID WE'VE RUN OUT OF FUEL!

AT LEAST WE GOT AS FAR AS DRY LAN—

CRACK!

CHOOFF!

WE... WE'RE UNHARMED! BUT WE'VE LOST HELPER!

THE ISLAND APPEARS TO BE RIDDLED WITH MANY VARYING LANDSCAPES! THIS REGION RESEMBLES THE HIMALAYAS!

I ALMOST FORGOT! I'VE STILL GOT THE PARCHMENT THAT MECHANICAL FAIRY DROPPED! IT'S ADDRESSED TO THE TWO OF US! AND IT'S FROM...

I DON'T BELIEVE IT! *MICKEY* AND *DONALD!*

THEY SAY WE'RE NEEDED ON MYTHOS ISLAND! AND THE CO-ORDINATES THEY'VE SUPPLIED...

...EXACTLY MATCH THE POSITION OF *THIS* ISLAND!

MYTHOS ISLAND, EH?! THOSE CREATURES WE SAW *DID* LOOK STRANGE, BUT WHO BELIEVES IN CENTAURS AND DRAGONS AND...

YETI!!

EXACTLY! THE ABOMINABLE SNOWMAN IS NOTHING BUT A FIGMENT OF THE...

WHAAA!!!

HURRY, GYRO! OVER HERE!

MY ROCKET IS PREPARED FOR ANY EMERGENCY! THE ROOF CONVERTS TO A SLED!

CLEVER, DOC!

CLICK!

SNAP!

GRR-OOURGH!

I HAVEN'T DONE THIS SINCE I WAS A KID!

AAAIIIEEEE!!!

UH-OH!

I'VE GOT A BAD FEELING ABOUT THIS!

SWOOOSH!!

YOW! THIS BIG BOY IS *FAST!*

UHF!! YOU CAN SAY *THAT* AGAIN!

IN THE AIR ABOVE, THE MEAN ROBOT IN THE FLYING ROCK HAS DISCOVERED HELPER...

"MIGHTOS! DON'T!!" CRIES AIRY THE MECHANICAL FAIRY...

BEEEZ!!

THOK!!

BUT SHE MANAGES TO SAVE HIM...

SWISH!

GRAB!

"SOMETHING'S WRONG WITH MIGHTOS!" AIRY EXPLAINS. "WE USED TO BE BEST FRIENDS! BUT HE'S CHANGED AND BECOME VERY MEAN!"

BZZ-BEEEEP...

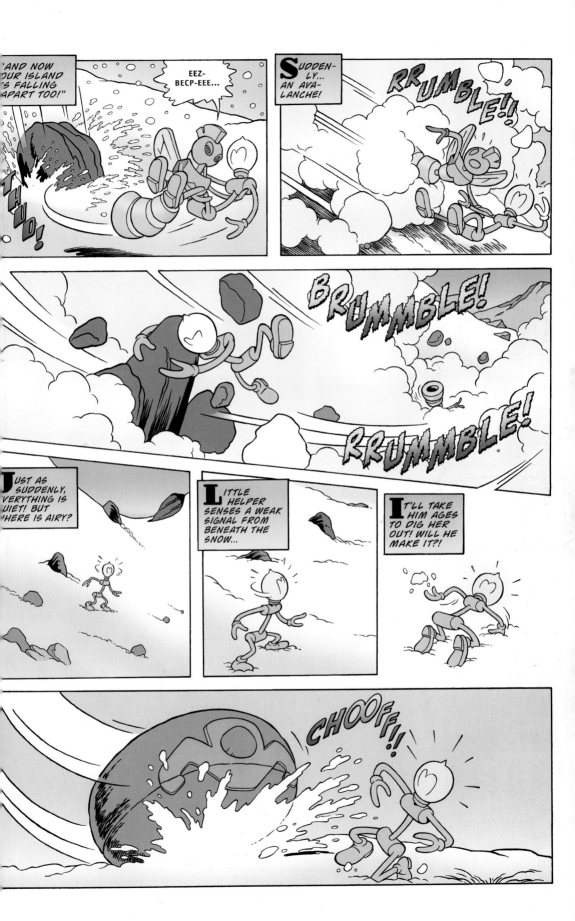

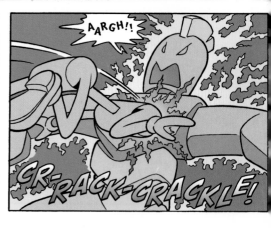

Meanwhile...

HEY, EVERY-BODY! DOC AND GYRO ARE HERE AT LAST!

ALL OUR FRIENDS! ARE THEY EXPECTING US TO FREE THEM?

CAN'T THEY SEE THAT WE'VE BEEN CAPTURED TOO?

DON'T WORRY! THE YETI'S JUST AS FRIENDLY AS EVERYONE ELSE HERE!

WE'RE *STUCK* ON THIS ISLAND BUT WE'RE NOT PRISONERS!

WE WEREN'T EVEN SUPPOSED TO BE HERE IN THE FIRST PLACE!

THE LETTERS THAT LED US TO THIS ROCK PILE WERE *REALLY* INTENDED FOR YOU GUYS!

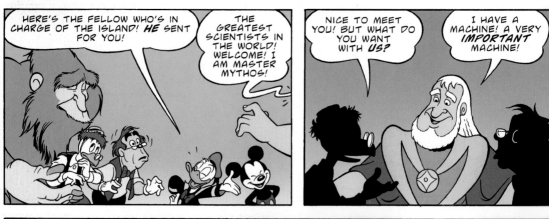

HERE'S THE FELLOW WHO'S IN CHARGE OF THE ISLAND! *HE* SENT FOR YOU!

THE GREATEST SCIENTISTS IN THE WORLD! WELCOME! I AM MASTER MYTHOS!

NICE TO MEET YOU! BUT WHAT DO YOU WANT WITH *US?*

I HAVE A MACHINE! A VERY *IMPORTANT* MACHINE!

IT NEEDS *FIXING!*

I'LL SAY!

BUT... WHAT'S IT *FOR?!*

THIS ISLE IS HOME TO ALL MYTHOLOGICAL CREATURES AND FROM TIME TO TIME, MY MACHINE SENT THEM TO YOUR WORLD FOR BRIEF VISITS!

YOU KNOW! WHEN SOMEONE THINKS THEY SAW A TROLL UNDER THE BRIDGE BY THEIR HOUSE OR A UNICORN IN THEIR GARDEN!

JUST A QUICK GLIMPSE! BUT ENOUGH TO MAKE ONE BELIEVE THEY *MIGHT* REALLY EXIST!

THEN PEOPLE TELL STORIES ABOUT THEM! AND THAT'S WHAT KEEPS THE MYTHS *ALIVE!*

WHAT WOULD THE WORLD BE WITHOUT MYTHS AND FAIRY TALES?

PURTY *BORIN'*, THET'S FER SURE!

AMAZING! IN ESSENCE, THIS MACHINE WAS A MATTER TRANSPORTER! BUT WHAT RUINED IT?!

MIGHTOS!

AT LAST, AIRY! YOU CONVINCED HIM TO RETURN! HE'S BACK TO NORMAL!

HELPER!

I CREATED MIGHTOS AND AIRY TO BE MY HELPERS! BUT THINGS BEGAN TO UPSET MIGHTOS AND IT ANNOYED HIM THAT...

...PEOPLE WEREN'T INTERESTED IN MYTHS ANYMORE! THEY'D FOUND OTHER THINGS...LIKE MAKING MONEY! AND WATCHING TV!

MIGHTOS FELT IT WAS HUMILIATING THAT WE CONTINUED SENDING OUR *BEAUTIFUL* FRIENDS TO YOUR WORLD! THAT PEOPLE DIDN'T DESERVE IT!

"THIS THOUGHT OBSESSED AND DARKENED HIS MIND! IT BLOCKED HIS USUAL SOUND THINKING! HE GOT MAD..."

"...AND DESTROYED THE MACHINE!"

CRASH!

HE DIDN'T REALIZE THE VERY *EXISTENCE* OF THE ISLAND DEPENDS ON THE CREATURES BEING SEEN IN THE REAL WORLD!

SO THAT'S WHY THE ISLAND IS CRUMBLING AWAY!

IF IT VANISHES COMPLETELY, ALL THE MYTHS OF THE EARTH WILL DISAPPEAR...

...FOREVER!

AND ALL OF *US* AS WELL! UNLESS, THAT IS, THESE GENTLEMEN CAN SAVE THE DAY!

DOC STATIC! GYRO GEARLOOSE! YOU *MUST* REPAIR MY MACHINE POSTHASTE! YOU'RE OUR ONLY HOPE!

SHEESH! WE COULDN'T EVEN GET OUR *OWN* MATTER TRANSPORTERS TO WORK BUT... WHAT THE HECK! I'LL GIVE IT THE OLD COLLEGE TRY!

WE'VE NEVER TEAMED UP ON AN INVENTION BEFORE, GYRO! MAYBE TWO HEADS *ARE* BETTER THAN ONE!

THAT'S THE SPIRIT, MEN! NOW GET TO WORK! WE'RE ALL COUNTING ON YOU!

Concluded in next issue...